weird but true! 8

weird but true! 8

350 OUTRAGEOUS FACTS

NATIONAL GEOGRAPHIC
WASHINGTON, D.C.

An **earthquake** made **Mount Everest** about an **inch shorter.**

(2.5 cm)

4

There are as many molecules in **ten drops** of **water** as there are **stars** in the **universe.**

KANGAROOS USE THEIR TAILS AS AN EXTRA LEG WHEN WALKING.

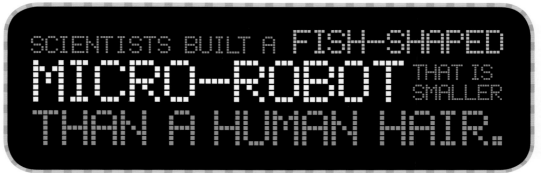

SCIENTISTS BUILT A FISH-SHAPED MICRO-ROBOT THAT IS SMALLER THAN A HUMAN HAIR.

A **FARMER** FROM MASSACHUSETTS, U.S.A., **ONCE PADDLED DOWN A RIVER IN AN 817-POUND** (371-kg) **HOLLOWED-OUT PUMPKIN.**

MORE PEOPLE ARE KILLED EACH YEAR BY DOMESTIC PIGS THAN BY SHARKS.

A compound in **human spit** can help **heal wounds.**

Scientists use a **barfing machine** and fake vomit to help them study how **viruses** spread through the air.

The planet Mercury is shrinking.

9

LUKE SKYWALKER'S **LIGHTSABER** HAS ACTUALLY BEEN TO **SPACE.**

ONE MAN OWNS 500,000 PIECES OF *STAR WARS*

The sound of **Darth Vader's breathing** was inspired by breathing apparatuses used for **scuba diving.**

A WATERFALL IN MINNESOTA, U.S.A., DROPS INTO A DEEP HOLE AND DISAPPEARS.

A GIANT BLACK HOLE ATE A STAR AND BURPED OUT A FLAME.

SOME OF THE EARLIEST BOATS WERE MADE FROM PLANTS.

Dragonflies can fly straight up and down and hover in midair like a helicopter.

A NOW EXTINCT FROG SPECIES SWALLOWED ITS EGGS, INCUBATED THEM IN ITS STOMACH, AND GAVE BIRTH THROUGH ITS MOUTH.

MOST MAMMALS HEAVIER THAN **6.6 POUNDS** (3 kg) TAKE THE SAME AMOUNT OF TIME TO **PEE.**

SOME **DIAMONDS** FALL **TO EARTH** FROM **OUTER SPACE**

Plants talk to one another through an underground network of fungi.

YOU NEED A **FOOT-LONG STICK,** (0.3-m) A **THREE-POUND PUCK,** (1.4-kg) AND **SNORKEL GEAR** TO **PLAY UNDERWATER HOCKEY.**

ONLY ABOUT **10** PERCENT OF THE POPULATION IS LEFT-HANDED.

Drinking *coffee* in 17th-century **Turkey** *was punishable* by **death.**

YOUR BODY'S SMELL—OR "ODORPRINT"—IS AS UNIQUE AS YOUR FINGERPRINTS.

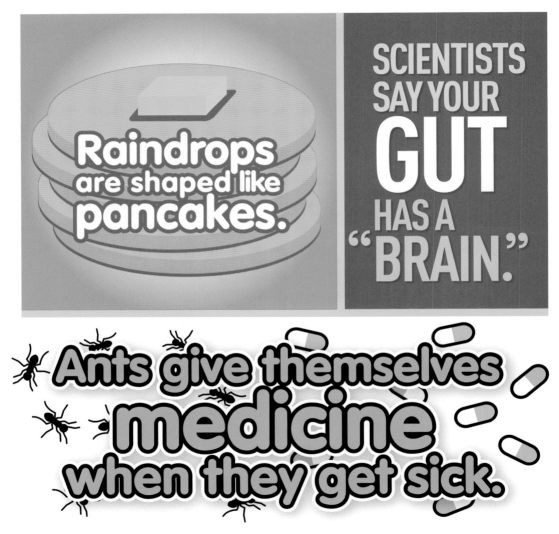

Raindrops are shaped like pancakes.

SCIENTISTS SAY YOUR GUT HAS A "BRAIN."

Ants give themselves medicine when they get sick.

20

Lightning almost never strikes the North or South Poles.

LIGHTNING **STRIKES** MEN MORE OFTEN THAN IT DOES WOMEN.

NEWBORN TASMANIAN DEVILS ARE THE SIZE OF A RAISIN.

Jellyfish invasions have shut down nuclear power plants.

There's an app that lets people **rent** out their **toilets.**

SCIENTISTS FOUND **PREHISTORIC VIRUSES** IN **SIBERIAN ICE.**

A 16th-century *astronomer* lost part of his **nose** in a duel about *math.*

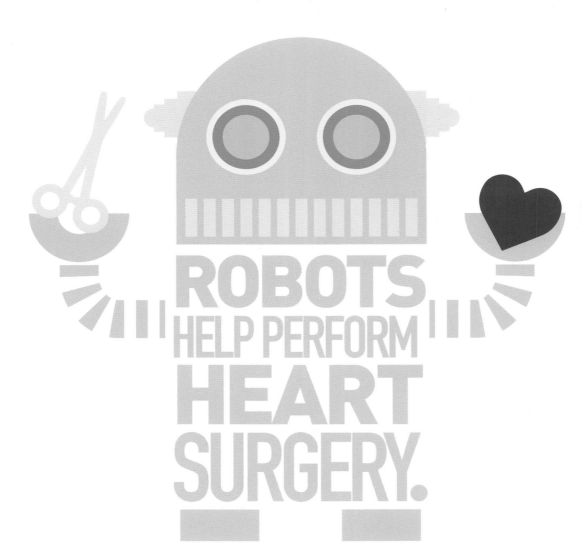

ROBOTS HELP PERFORM HEART SURGERY.

THE HUBBLE SPACE TELESCOPE CAN LOOK BACK IN TIME.

Mushrooms are also called toadstools.

NEANDERTHALS FLOSSED THEIR TEETH WITH TWIGS AND BLADES OF GRASS.

peecycling = using urine to fertilize vegetables

RESEARCHERS HAVE DEVELOPED **3-D GLASSES** FOR **INSECTS.**

A STUDY FOUND THAT CHILDREN WHOSE FAMILIES WASH DISHES BY HAND HAVE FEWER ALLERGIES THAN KIDS WHOSE FAMILIES USE A DISHWASHER.

Wolf pups can't see or hear when they're born.

You are made of star dust.

Some plants can hear themselves being eaten.

There was only **one student in** New Mexico State University's first graduating class.

There are approximately **3 trillion** (3,000,000,000,000) trees on Earth.

ONE RARE PLANT GROWS ONLY ON TOP OF DIAMOND DEPOSITS.

THAT'S WEIRD!

A **BROWN BAT** CAN EAT **1,000 MOSQUITOES** IN AN HOUR.

People in one small Turkish town communicate over long distances by **whistling.**

A MAN SUED THE KELLOGG COMPANY BECAUSE HE FOUND NO REAL FRUIT IN HIS FROOT LOOPS CEREAL.

SCIENTISTS THINK **T. REX** WAS A CANNIBAL.

Some **carnivorous plants can eat** birds.

During his 1905 U.S. presidential inauguration, *Teddy Roosevelt* **wore** *a ring* containing a lock of **Abraham Lincoln's** *hair.*

Your brain produces enough energy to power a small lightbulb.

HUMMINGBIRDS USE **HAWKS** FOR PROTECTION.

moonbow=

a nighttime rainbow

Early **rugby balls** were made from **inflated pigs' bladders.**

2015 was the International Year of Light.

SCIENTISTS HAVE DISCOVERED A PROTEIN THAT CAN PREVENT **ICE CREAM** FROM **MELTING** QUICKLY IN HOT WEATHER.

THE BOARD GAME MONOPOLY

WAS ORIGINALLY CALLED THE LANDLORD'S GAME.

MONOPOLY IS BASED ON **STREET NAMES** IN ATLANTIC CITY, NEW JERSEY, U.S.A.

THE AVERAGE PERSON EATS **2,500** CALORIES AT THANKSGIVING DINNER.

Scientists who are Star Wars fans nicknamed a new species of ape the Skywalker hoolock gibbon.

There is NO WORD in the English language that RHYMES WITH "**month.**"

GRIMA = THE FEELING YOU GET WHEN YOU HEAR **FINGERNAILS** ON A CHALKBOARD

NASA found evidence that **one of** Saturn's moons has an energy source that may be able to support life.

Scientists found **152-million-year-old crocodile eggs** in Portugal.

Musicians have slightly **faster reaction times** than **nonmusicians,** a study found.

THERE IS A PLANT CALLED **JACK-GO-TO-BED-AT-NOON.**

Citizens of the town of Onoway, Canada, once had **PINK TAP WATER.**

Eels use Earth's magnetic field **to navigate.**

SCIENTISTS CREATED **ARTIFICIAL SKIN** THAT CAN **SENSE TEMPERATURE CHANGES.**

UPS drivers **hardly** ever make **left turns.**

In **6.7** million **years, a day will be** ONE MINUTE **LONGER.**

That's Weird!

Parrots, sea anemones, and mussels **don't toot.**

(But bats, hedgehogs, and snakes do.)

45

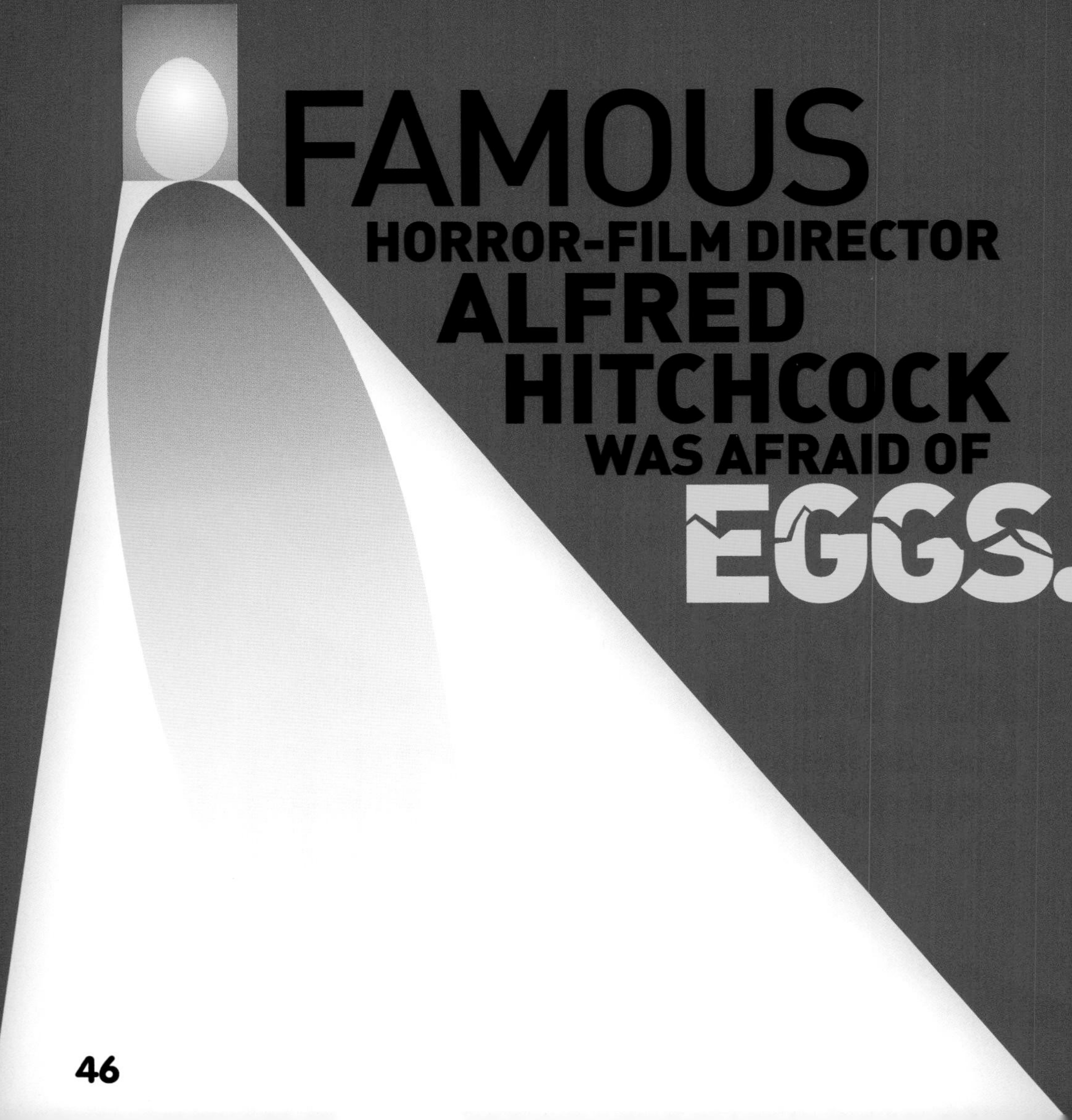

FAMOUS

HORROR-FILM DIRECTOR

ALFRED
HITCHCOCK

WAS AFRAID OF

EGGS.

U.S. president James A. Garfield was fond of squirrel soup.

FEMALE PHARAOHS WORE FAKE BEARDS.

Scientists made medicine out of cockroach brain cells.

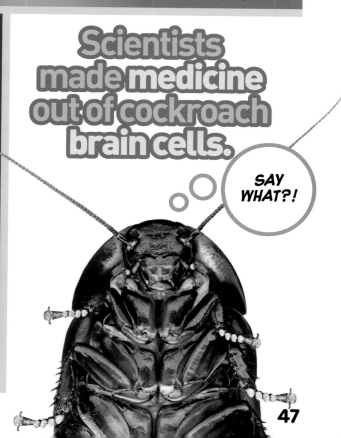

SAY WHAT?!

Elephants "have fingers" on the end of their trunks.

POPE LEO X **BURIED** HIS

SOME OF AN ELEPHANT'S **TEETH** ARE THE SIZE OF A BRICK.

PET ELEPHANT **UNDER** THE VATICAN.

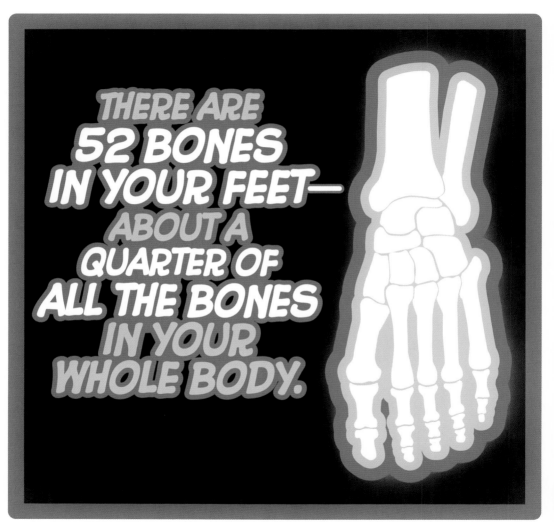

THERE ARE 52 BONES IN YOUR FEET—ABOUT A QUARTER OF ALL THE BONES IN YOUR WHOLE BODY.

VANILLA IS USED TO MAKE CHOCOLATE.

Some **dogs' paws** smell like corn chips.

AFTER THEIR 1972 NATIONAL HOCKEY LEAGUE WIN,

THE BOSTON BRUINS'S NAME WAS MISSPELLED "BQSTQN BRUINS" ON THE STANLEY CUP.

THERE'S A ROCK ON MARS THAT LOOKS LIKE A FLOATING SPOON.

AN EAR OF CORN CAN HAVE UP TO 1,200 KERNELS.

A LIBROCUBICULARIST IS SOMEONE WHO READS IN BED.

Police "arrested" a goat for loitering outside a doughnut shop in Saskatchewan, Canada.

There are more than 40,000 types of rice.

If you strung together all the **cranberries** grown in North America **in one year,** they would stretch from Boston to Los Angeles, U.S.A., more than **500 times.**

SHEEP SHEARING IS A COMPETITIVE SPORT.

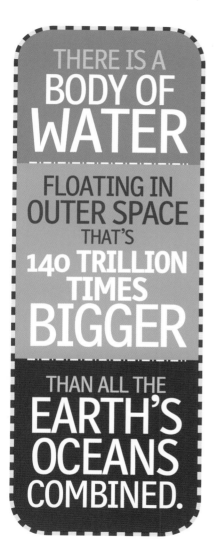

THERE IS A **BODY OF WATER** FLOATING IN OUTER SPACE THAT'S **140 TRILLION TIMES BIGGER** THAN ALL THE **EARTH'S OCEANS** COMBINED.

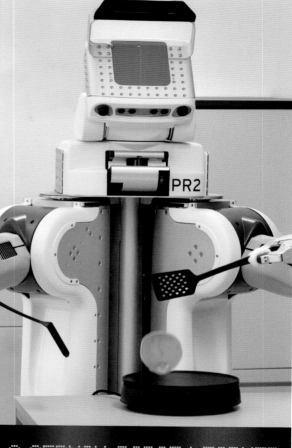

A GERMAN ROBOT LEARNED HOW TO MAKE PANCAKES.

penny farthing= a bicycle with a giant **front wheel** and a tiny back wheel

TOMATOES CAN BE PURPLE.

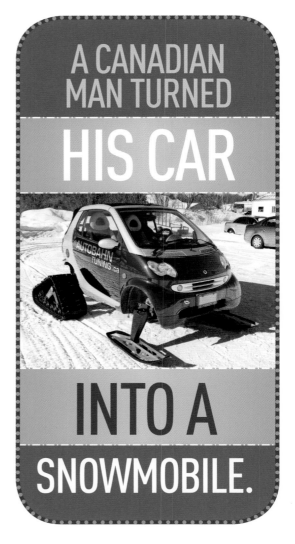

A CANADIAN MAN TURNED

HIS CAR

INTO A

SNOWMOBILE.

Fastest
one-mile run
(1.6-km)
by a human
wearing swim fins:
5 minutes and
48.86 seconds

During Olympic training, **swimmer** Michael Phelps consumed more than **12,000 calories** a day—about the equivalent of **80 cups of whole milk.** (18.9 L)

CHRISTOPHER COLUMBUS BROUGHT THE FIRST **LEMON SEEDS** TO THE AMERICAS.

PARTS OF CALIFORNIA, U.S.A., ARE SINKING.

IN NEW ZEALAND, PARENTS AREN'T ALLOWED TO NAME THEIR BABIES AFTER PUNCTUATION MARKS.

" ! ? ; - , (:) [,] ' { . . . }.

A HONEYBEE HAS THE SAME NUMBER OF HAIRS AS A SQUIRREL: THREE MILLION.

SCIENTISTS ARE DEVELOPING ROBOT BEES

HONEY
HAS BEEN FOUND
IN THE
CENTER OF OLD
GOLF BALLS.

THAT COULD ARTIFICIALLY POLLINATE CROPS.

There's a **comet** shaped like a **rubber duck.**

CHOCOLATE WAS ONCE USED AS MONEY.

Some **snakes pass gas** in self-defense.

Painting was once an Olympic event.

One in four medicines comes from rain forest plants.

The world's first speeding **ticket** was given to a motorist going **eight miles** an hour. (12.9 km/h)

The 1904 World's Fair featured a life-size elephant made of almonds.

BACTERIA TALK TO EACH OTHER.

"chicken wing" = a bad golf swing

The city of Redondo Beach, California, U.S.A., once chose a **blimp** as its **official bird.**

SNAILS SMELL WITH THEIR LIPS.

TO ENSURE THEY HAVEN'T BEEN SWITCHED OR TAMPERED WITH, ALL EGGS USED IN THE COMPETITIVE SPORT OF EGG THROWING ARE MARKED FOR SECURITY PURPOSES.

"FRIED EGG"=THE WAY A GOLF

SCIENTISTS HAVE FIGURED OUT HOW TO UNBOIL AN EGG.

BALL SOMETIMES LANDS IN A SAND TRAP

Humans and dogs perform together in a sport called musical canine freestyle.

Einstein never wore socks.

Earmuffs *were* invented by a *teenage boy* in 1858.

Some **ORCHIDS** smell like human body odor to attract **mosquitoes.**

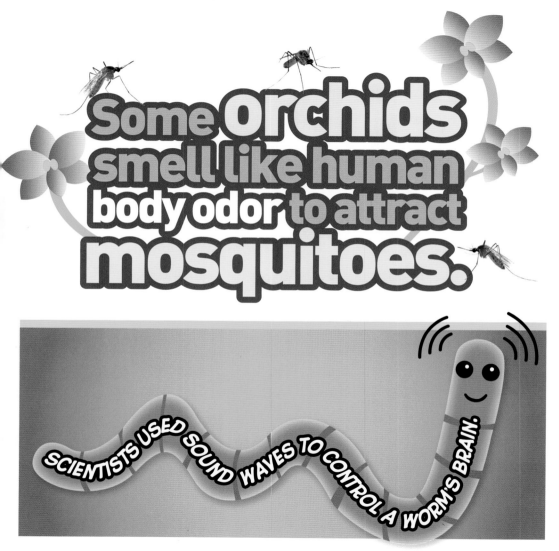

SCIENTISTS USED SOUND WAVES TO CONTROL A WORM'S BRAIN.

DEATH METAL MUSIC ATTRACTS SHARKS.

IN NEW ZEALAND, YOU CAN **PLAY GOLF** WITH **FOOTBALL-SHAPED GOLF BALLS.**

Some scientists think that **plants** can learn.

Spiders can build **webs** that are a half mile long.

(0.8 km)

An artist created an **18-foot-long** (5.5-m) **Batmobile** out of more than **500,000** Lego bricks.

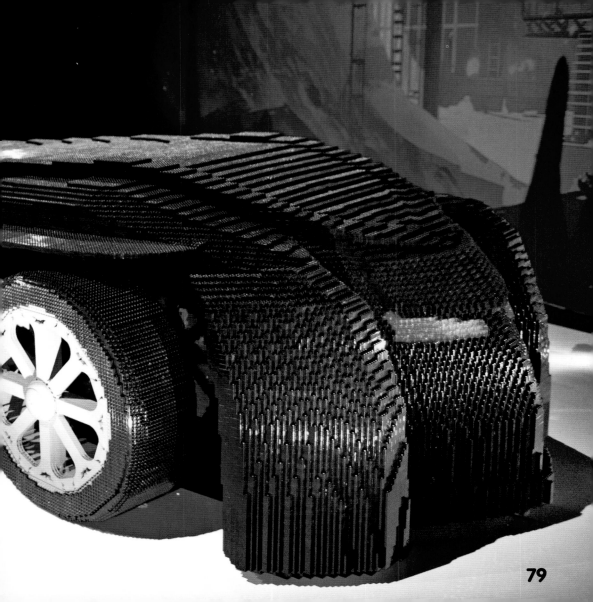

Tooth enamel evolved from ancient fish scales.

An aglet is the plastic piece at the end of your shoelace.

Fidgeting can make you healthier.

snood = the flesh that hangs down over a male turkey's beak

THE LONGEST
PIZZA

EVER MADE
WAS ALMOST A
MILE LONG.
(1.6 km)

IT WAS MADE WITH

1.5 TONS
(1.4 t) OF

MOZZARELLA
AND

2 TONS OF
(1.8 t)

TOMATO SAUCE.

GLOBAL WARMING IS CHANGING THE SHAPE OF THE PLANET.

Kids grow faster in the springtime.

The **SLIME** of a frog found in southern India contains molecules that **CAN KILL THE FLU VIRUS.**

BIRD POOP HELPS FIGHT CLIMATE CHANGE **BY COOLING** DOWN **THE ARCTIC.**

People in a New Zealand town **built a tunnel** so the **penguins** that live there could **safely cross** under a busy road.

PENGUIN CROSSING

SOME WORMS CAN "TASTE" SUNLIGHT.

A species of ant in sub-Saharan Africa **rescues its wounded comrades** from battles with termites.

THE EASTER BUNNY SKYDIVED INTO A NEIGHBORHOOD IN CORPUS CHRISTI, TEXAS, U.S.A.

SCIENTISTS FOUND THE FOSSIL OF A **120-MILLION-** YEAR-OLD **FLYING DINOSAUR** WITH IRIDESCENT FEATHERS.

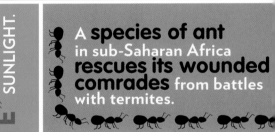

Coconut crabs **pinch harder than** grizzly bears bite.

YELLOW TAXIS GET INTO **FEWER ACCIDENTS** THAN *BLUE ONES.*

A Minnesota, U.S.A., restaurant made a **100-pound** (45-kg) CHOCOLATE **EGG.**

Scientists invented a **SOLAR-POWERED DEVICE** that can **PULL WATER** from **DESERT AIR.**

That's Weird!

TALKING TO YOUR PUP IN A HIGH-PITCHED **"BABY VOICE"** HELPS IT PAY ATTENTION, **A STUDY FOUND.**

Bonobos **blOw** raspberries for attention.

LISTENING TO ROCK MUSIC WHILE EATING CAN MAKE FOOD TASTE SPICIER, ONE STUDY FOUND.

In China you can order dried-pork-and-seaweed-**flavored doughnuts.**

SOME **BABY SPIDERS** EAT THEIR **MOTHER.**

Computers can be programmed to recognize emotions in stories.

88

A **FROG** NAMED SANTJIE MADE THE **LONGEST** RECORDED JUMP— **33 FEET** 5.5 INCHES (10.2 m) AT A FROG DERBY IN **SOUTH AFRICA**.

The stringy parts of a **banana** are called **phloem** (FLO-em).

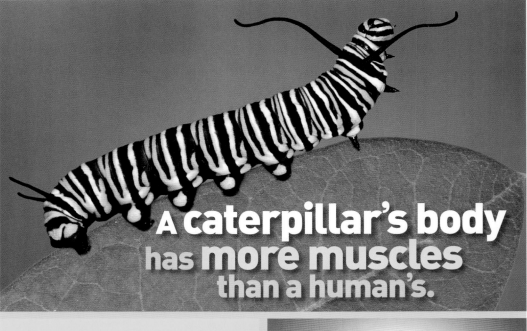

A **caterpillar's body** has **more muscles** than a human's.

baboon = a type of lemon

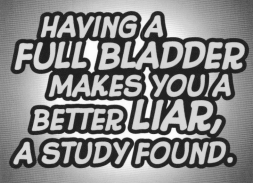

HAVING A FULL BLADDER MAKES YOU A BETTER LIAR, A STUDY FOUND.

ONE OF MARS'S MOONS IS FALLING APART.

Prairie dogs say **hello** with **kisses.**

VIRGA IS RAIN THAT EVAPORATES BEFORE IT HITS THE GROUND.

PLANTS CAN GET FEVERS.

A man named **Santa Claus** once ran for city council in North Pole, Alaska, U.S.A.

The average **tornado** is on the ground for only **five minutes.**

King Henry III of England had a **pet bear** that swam in the Thames River and caught fish.

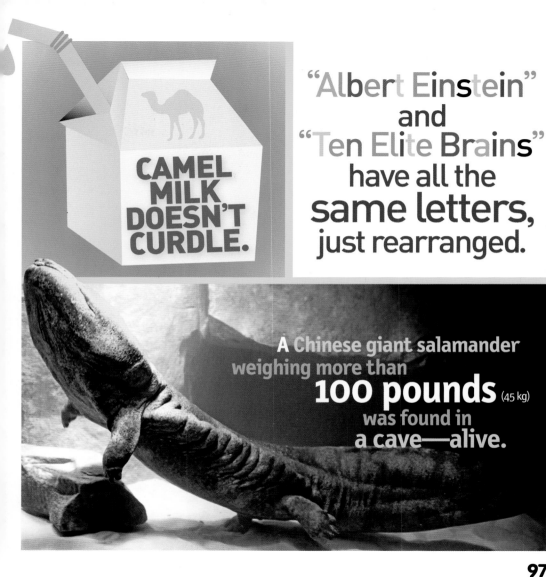

CAMEL MILK DOESN'T CURDLE.

"Albert Einstein" and "Ten Elite Brains" have all the same letters, just rearranged.

A Chinese giant salamander weighing more than **100 pounds** (45 kg) was found in a cave—alive.

An **artist** covered an entire **city bus** with **yarn.**

Jousting *is the* *official sport*

of the U.S. state of Maryland.

PUMPKINS ALMOST WENT EXTINCT.

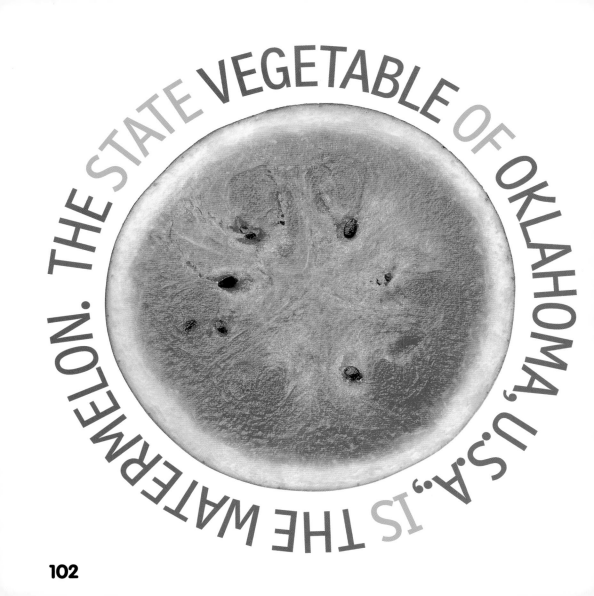

THE STATE VEGETABLE OF OKLAHOMA, U.S.A., IS THE WATERMELON.

The U.S. state of **Kansas** produces enough **wheat** every year to make **36 billion** loaves of bread.

HUMANS HAVE EXPLORED LESS

THAN 5 PERCENT OF THE OCEAN.

earworm = a song that gets stuck in your head

The first living things on Earth were **bacteria.**

DOMINOES' SPOTS ARE CALLED PIPS.

A man in Spain has ribs made by a 3-D printer.

THE SUN SOMETIMES HAS HOLES IN IT.

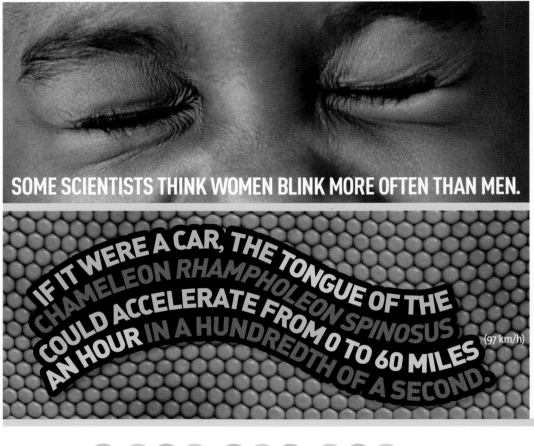

SOME SCIENTISTS THINK WOMEN BLINK MORE OFTEN THAN MEN.

IF IT WERE A CAR, THE TONGUE OF THE CHAMELEON RHAMPHOLEON SPINOSUS COULD ACCELERATE FROM 0 TO 60 MILES AN HOUR IN A HUNDREDTH OF A SECOND.

(97 km/h)

ABOUT **9,000,000,000** PIECES OF

CANDY CORN WILL BE MADE THIS YEAR.

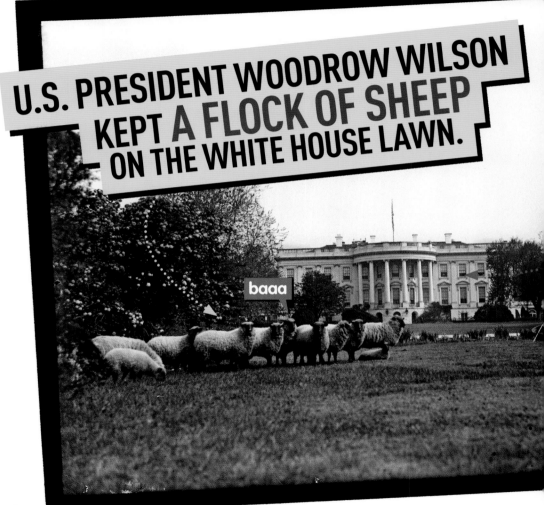

U.S. PRESIDENT WOODROW WILSON KEPT A FLOCK OF SHEEP ON THE WHITE HOUSE LAWN.

baaa

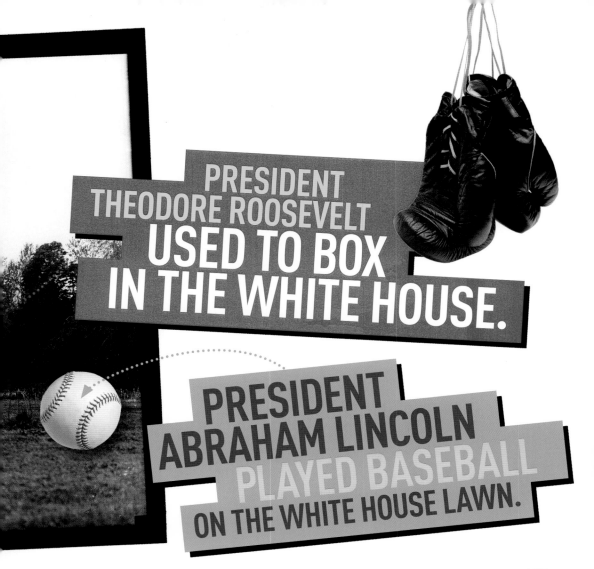

PRESIDENT THEODORE ROOSEVELT **USED TO BOX IN THE WHITE HOUSE.**

PRESIDENT ABRAHAM LINCOLN PLAYED BASEBALL ON THE WHITE HOUSE LAWN.

SNAKES ONCE HAD LEGS.

A U.S. UNIVERSITY HAS THOUSANDS OF **BRAINS** STORED IN A **BRAIN BANK.**

The most expensive car ever sold went for $35.7 million.

The **sea bunny** is actually **a slug.**

PLUTO IS ONLY ABOUT HALF AS WIDE AS THE UNITED STATES.

YOUR TASTE BUDS GO NUMB WHEN YOU FLY.

AMERICA'S FIRST ROLLER COASTER HAULED COAL IN THE MORNING AND PEOPLE IN THE AFTERNOON.

RESEARCHERS FOUND A NEW SPECIES OF **SPIDER THAT PLAYS PEEKABOO TO ATTRACT MATES.**

ONLY ONE PERCENT OF ALL THE WATER ON EARTH IS FIT FOR HUMAN USE.

No one really knows why **humans** have to **sleep.**

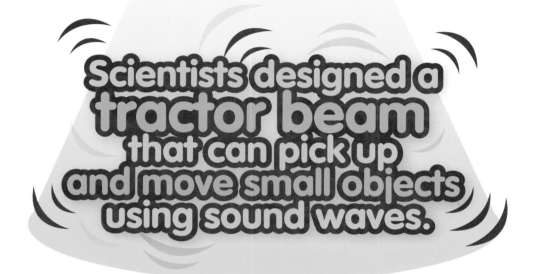

Scientists designed a **tractor beam** that can pick up and move small objects using sound waves.

THE EARTH IS MOVING AWAY FROM THE SUN.

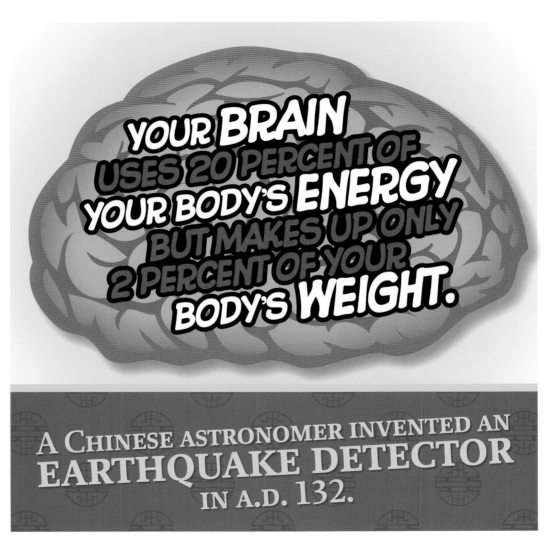

YOUR **BRAIN** USES 20 PERCENT OF YOUR BODY'S **ENERGY** BUT MAKES UP ONLY 2 PERCENT OF YOUR BODY'S **WEIGHT.**

A CHINESE ASTRONOMER INVENTED AN **EARTHQUAKE DETECTOR** IN A.D. 132.

ONE SPECIES OF BIRD "TAP DANCES" TO ATTRACT A MATE.

I'VE GOT DANCIN' FEET!

A ten-gallon cowboy hat holds only three quarts of water. (2.8 L)

SOUR PATCH KIDS WERE ORIGINALLY CALLED MARS MEN.

AUTOMOBILES ARE THE

MOST **RECYCLED PRODUCT**
IN THE UNITED STATES.

There are about **3.4 trillion** gallons (13 trillion L) of water in **Earth's** atmosphere.

A **650-YEAR-OLD** TEMPLE WAS DISCOVERED **UNDER A SUPERMARKET** IN MEXICO CITY.

SOME SCIENTISTS WANT TO SPRAY GLACIERS WITH ARTIFICIAL SNOW TO KEEP THEM FROM **SHRINKING.**

SCIENTISTS UNCOVERED FOSSILS FROM AN **ANCIENT GOOSELIKE BIRD** THAT WAS **FIVE FEET** (1.5 M) **TALL** AND WEIGHED **48 POUNDS** (22 KG).

FIREFIGHTERS IN DUBAI, U.A.E., WEAR **WATER-POWERED JET PACKS** TO FIGHT FIRES FROM THE AIR.

Dorado catfish migrate the length of the Amazon River and back: **7,200 miles** (11,587 km). (That's nearly the entire width of South America!)

CITY BIRDS ARE BETTER AT SOLVING PROBLEMS THAN **COUNTRY BIRDS, A STUDY FOUND.**

THE WORLD'S **FASTEST FLYING** CREATURE IS A **BAT.**

The **Sand Museum** in Tottori, Japan, featured a **model** of MOUNT RUSHMORE crafted from about **3,000 tons** (2,722 t) OF SAND.

Doctors once found **150 worms** living inside a woman's stomach.

NAKED MOLE RATS CAN SURVIVE WITHOUT OXYGEN FOR **18 MINUTES.**

That's Weird!

125

POODLES ARE **BANNED** FROM COMPETING IN THE **IDITAROD.**

The world's heaviest **turnip** weighed as much as a four-year-old **kid.**

THE AVERAGE AMERICAN EATS ABOUT A TON OF FOOD EACH YEAR. (0.9 t)

SCIENTISTS MADE A BATTERY USING MUSHROOMS.

The largest **muscle** in your body is your **gluteus** maximus— in your rear end.

127

An Australian man once tried to auction off the country of New Zealand online.

Too much **oxygen** can make **you sick.**

GRAB A BITE IN ONE OF THESE U.S. TOWNS:

OATMEAL, TEXAS

SANDWICH, MASSACHUSETTS

PIE TOWN, NEW MEXICO

BURNT CORN, ALABAMA

CHICKEN, ALASKA

COOKIETOWN, OKLAHOMA

You become temporarily **paralyzed** while you dream.

275 PEOPLE FIT INSIDE THE WORLD'S LARGEST SOAP BUBBLE.

HORSES DON'T THROW UP.

THE **SNICKERS BAR** WAS NAMED AFTER A HORSE.

Starburst candies were invented in the United Kingdom and were originally called Opal Fruits.

spitters *sneesl* *snaw*

THERE ARE MORE THAN 400 WORDS FOR SNOW IN SCOTLAND.

flindrikin *skelf* *unbrak* *feefle*

OCTOBER 9 IS NATIONAL MOLDY CHEESE DAY IN THE U.S.

★★★

An ancient *Chinese warrior* is said to have **stunned enemy troops** into retreat by *juggling nine balls* at once.

133

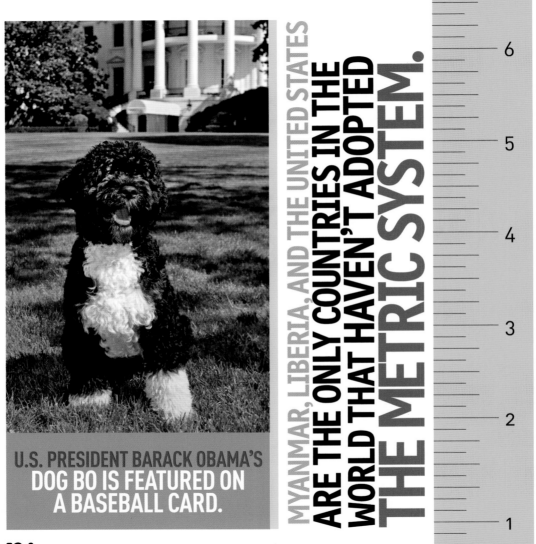

U.S. PRESIDENT BARACK OBAMA'S **DOG BO IS FEATURED ON A BASEBALL CARD.**

MYANMAR, LIBERIA, AND THE UNITED STATES **ARE THE ONLY COUNTRIES IN THE WORLD THAT HAVEN'T ADOPTED THE METRIC SYSTEM.**

Scientists found **sharks** living in an underwater **volcano**.

The entire land area of the **United States** could fit in the **Sahara desert**.

Some people in Ontario, Canada, **ice-skate to work.**

44,000 CANS OF SPAM ARE MADE EVERY HOUR.

PILOTS AND COPILOTS EAT DIFFERENT FOOD OFF THE IN-FLIGHT **MENU** IN CASE ONE OF THE MEALS MAKES **THEM SICK.**

Americans renamed **sauerkraut** "Liberty Cabbage" during World War I.

A WOMAN IN CHINA GREW HER **HAIR** THREE TIMES **LONGER** THAN SHE WAS **TALL.**

AN ANCIENT **FLYING REPTILE** HAD A WINGSPAN ABOUT AS WIDE AS A **FIGHTER JET.**

Chocolate comes from a fruit tree.

Arica, Chile, once went **14 years** with no **rainfall.**

New England **clam chowder** is the official state **dish of** Massachusetts, U.S.A.

The **oldest** **pieces of** **paper** in the world are **4,600** years old.

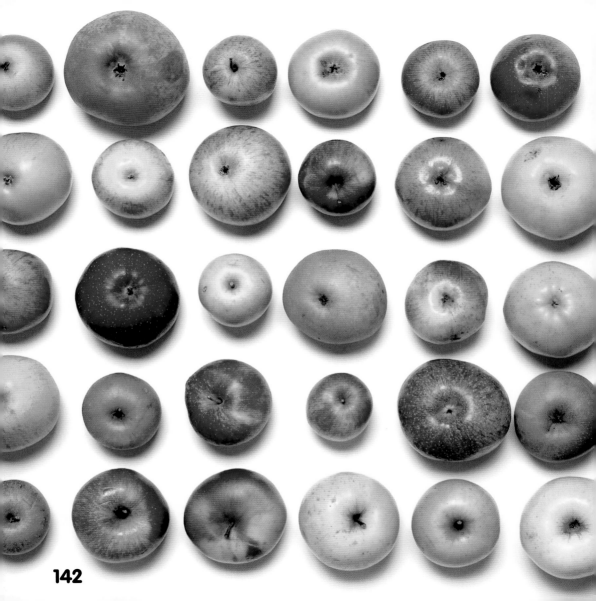

If you ate **one variety** of **apple per day,** it would take you almost **20 years** to try all the **different kinds.**

AMERICANS WILL EAT MORE THAN 6,000 PIECES OF PIZZA IN A LIFETIME.

The country of Tonga once had banana-shaped postage stamps.

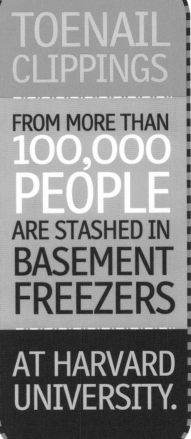

TOENAIL CLIPPINGS FROM MORE THAN 100,000 PEOPLE ARE STASHED IN BASEMENT FREEZERS AT HARVARD UNIVERSITY.

AN ARTIST ONCE RE-CREATED THE **"MONA LISA"** USING ONLY PIECES OF **TOAST.**

"EMOTION RECOGNITION" SOFTWARE DETERMINED THAT THE **"MONA LISA"** IS 83 PERCENT HAPPY, 9 PERCENT DISGUSTED, 6 PERCENT FEARFUL, AND 2 PERCENT ANGRY.

The **50-star American flag** was designed by a high school student. His teacher gave him a B minus.

DISNEYLAND, IN CALIFORNIA, U.S.A., IS BIGGER THAN THE WORLD'S SMALLEST COUNTRY.

SOME OF THE BIGGEST PYRAMIDS

IN THE WORLD ARE IN MEXICO.

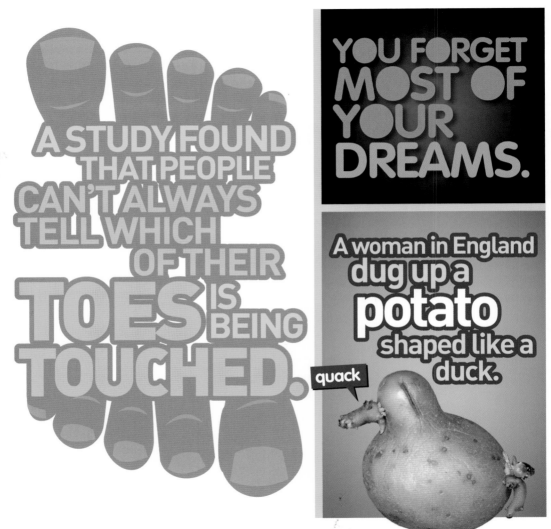

A STUDY FOUND THAT PEOPLE CAN'T ALWAYS TELL WHICH OF THEIR TOES IS BEING TOUCHED.

YOU FORGET MOST OF YOUR DREAMS.

A woman in England dug up a **potato** shaped like a duck.

quack

150

THREE AND A HALF TONS (3.2 t) OF **RED, WHITE, AND BLUE JELLY BEANS** WERE SHIPPED TO WASHINGTON, D.C., FOR U.S. PRESIDENT RONALD REAGAN'S 1981 INAUGURATION.

Dinosaurs may have **danced** to attract mates.

Some **turtles** **glow** in the dark.

PINK LEMONADE WAS INVENTED BY ACCIDENT, WHEN A LEMONADE SELLER DROPPED **RED CINNAMON CANDIES** INTO HIS LEMONADE, TURNING IT **PINK.**

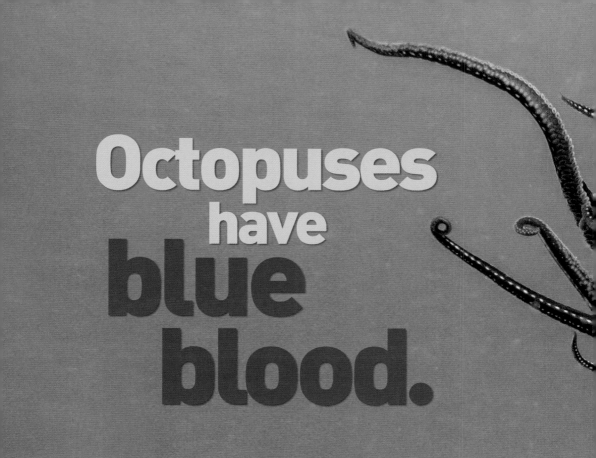

Octopuses
have
blue
blood.

OCTOPUSES CAN SEE WITH THEIR SKIN.

OCTOPUSES HAVE **NINE** BRAINS.

Giraffes **hum** at night.

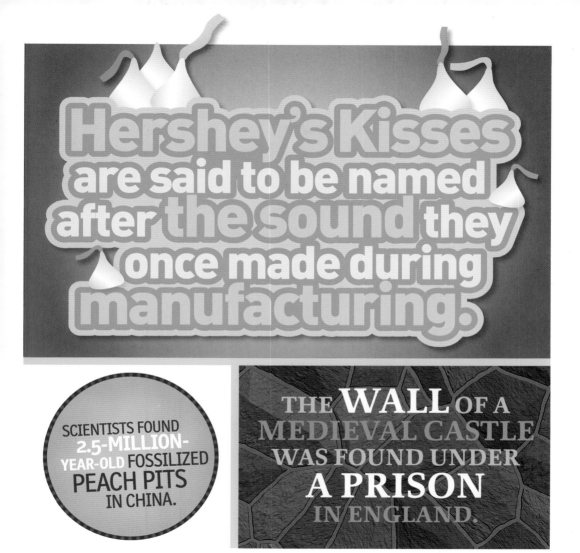

Hershey's Kisses are said to be named after the sound they once made during manufacturing.

SCIENTISTS FOUND **2.5-MILLION-YEAR-OLD** FOSSILIZED **PEACH PITS** IN CHINA.

THE **WALL** OF A MEDIEVAL CASTLE WAS FOUND UNDER **A PRISON** IN ENGLAND.

ONE AIRPLANE CAN CONTAIN 330 MILES OF WIRES. (531 km)

A fast-food chain once sold a **hamburger** that turned people's poop **green.**

More than **500 different** types of **bugs** may be living in your house, a study found.

Microlattice— the world's **lightest metal**— is **99.99** percent **air.**

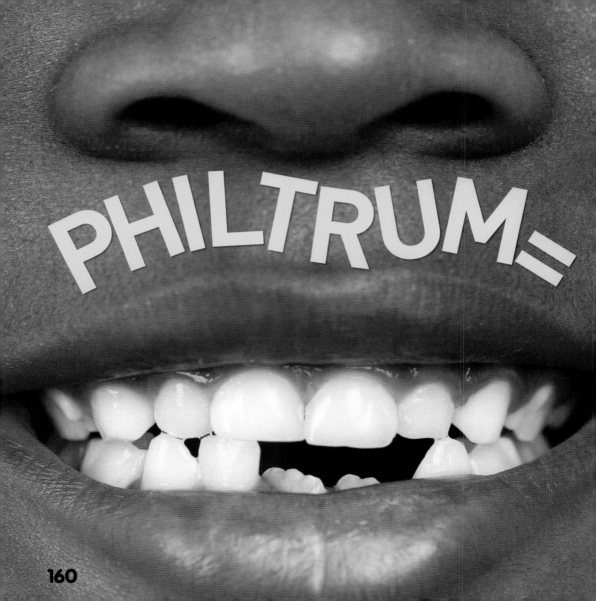

PHILTRUM=

THE **GROOVE** BETWEEN THE **TOP OF** YOUR **UPPER LIP** AND THE BOTTOM OF YOUR **NOSE**

AUSTRALIAN SCIENTISTS MADE SWIMSUITS FOR **SEA** TURTLES.

A truck carrying onions once caught fire near Frying Pan Road in Texas, U.S.A. (The driver got away safely.)

A WHALE FOSSIL WAS FOUND ON TOP OF A MOUNTAIN.

Some people are paid to **sniff** out the source of disgusting **smells.**

SCIENTISTS HOPE TO **SEND AN ORBITER** TO **EXPLORE** THE SKIES OF **VENUS IN 2025.**

SCIENTISTS RECENTLY DISCOVERED AN EXTINCT DOGLIKE PREDATOR THAT LIVED AROUND **30 MILLION** YEARS AGO.

"CORGI" IS WELSH FOR "DWARF DOG."

THERE ARE **12 SPECIES** OF **SPIDERS** THAT **EAT BIRDS.**

An **OCTOPUS** was washed into a parking garage **during a high tide** in Miami, Florida, U.S.A.

(It was rescued and returned to the ocean.)

Stethoscopes are also called **"guessing tubes**

MOST MAMMALS TAKE ONLY 12 SECONDS TO POOP.

164

SPACE HAMBURGER = THE DISK OF GAS AND DUST "FEEDING" A YOUNG STAR

People who regularly eat hot chili peppers **live longer** than people who don't, a study found.

The sentence **"The five boxing wizards jump quickly"** uses **every letter of the alphabet** at least once.

SCIENTISTS ARE **DEVELOPING** AN **ANTIBIOTIC** BASED ON **BLOOD** FROM A **KOMODO DRAGON**.

That's Weird!

CHIMPANZEES USE MAKESHIFT **FISHING RODS** TO GATHER ALGAE FROM RIVERS.

IT WOULD TAKE YOU ALMOST **SIX MONTHS** TO DRIVE A CAR FROM **EARTH TO THE MOON** AT **60 MILES AN HOUR.** (97 km/h)

TURKEYS WERE CONSIDERED SACRED BY EARLY NATIVE AMERICANS.

THERE WAS A COCKROACH HALL OF FAME IN PLANO, TEXAS, U.S.A.

Blue is the most popular toothbrush color.

IT TOOK UP TO **SEVEN PEOPLE TO OPERATE THE GIANT JABBA THE HUTT PUPPET** FROM THE *STAR WARS* MOVIES.

167

During a **drought,** the city of Los Angeles dropped **96 million plastic** **"shade balls"** into a reservoir to keep the water from evaporating.

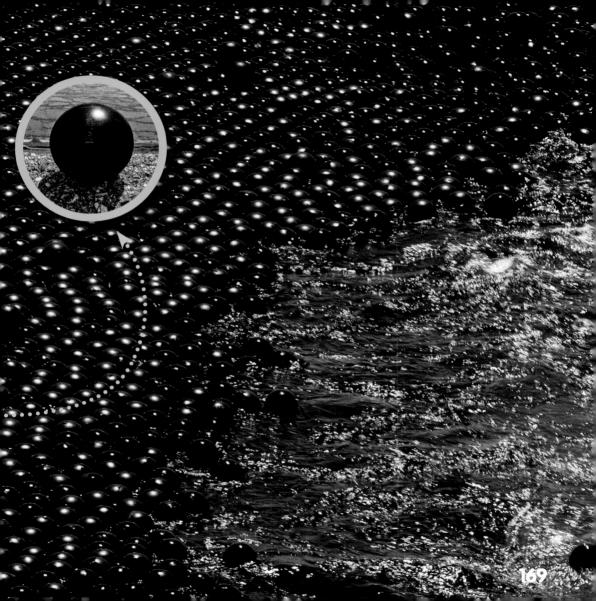

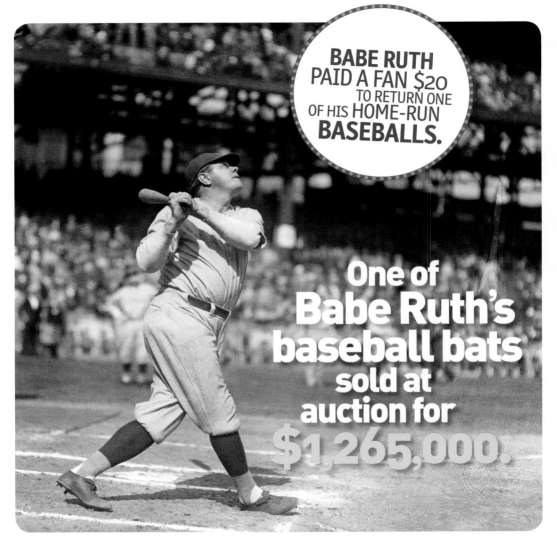

BABE RUTH PAID A FAN $20 TO RETURN ONE OF HIS **HOME-RUN BASEBALLS.**

One of **Babe Ruth's baseball bats** sold at auction for **$1,265,000.**

THE MOST HULA HOOPS SPUN AT ONE TIME: 200

A ROCK GROUP ONCE BANNED **BROWN M&M's** FROM BACKSTAGE AT THEIR CONCERTS.

SCIENTISTS HAVE TRAINED **PIGEONS** TO SPOT **CANCEROUS CELLS** ON MEDICAL IMAGES.

171

TAYLOR SWIFT DARE TO BE DIFFERENT 2015

A **FARM** IN MARYLAND, U.S.A., CREATED A **CORN MAZE** IN THE SHAPE OF SINGER TAYLOR SWIFT'S FACE.

SUMMERS FARM

AN ARTIST USED 17,625 GUMBALLS TO RE-CREATE TAYLOR SWIFT'S FACE.

Mantis shrimp send each other secret messages using light signals.

A lunch menu from the R.M.S. Titanic sold for **$88,000** in an online auction.

In Massachusetts, U.S.A., it is illegal to dance to "The Star-Spangled Banner."

WORMS THE SIZE OF **SNAKES** WERE FOUND ON A REMOTE **SCOTTISH ISLAND.**

MOST OF EARTH'S SPECIES ARE STILL UNDISCOVERED.

More than **100 baseballs** are used in one **Major League Baseball game.**

IT CAN TAKE UP TO 21 DAYS TO MAKE A SINGLE JELLY BEAN.

YOU CAN BUY EARMUFFS MADE FROM ROADKILL.

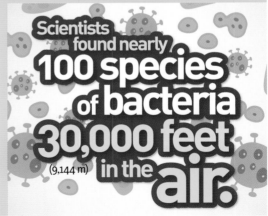

Scientists found nearly 100 species of bacteria 30,000 feet (9,144 m) in the air.

A STUDY FOUND THAT

CHILDREN WHO **GROW UP** AROUND **DOGS**

HAVE A LOWER RISK OF **ASTHMA** THAN KIDS WHO AREN'T EXPOSED TO DOGS.

BY 2050 THE OCEAN WILL CONTAIN MORE PLASTIC THAN FISH, ACCORDING TO ONE REPORT.

MICROBES IN YOUR GUT TELL YOUR BRAIN WHEN YOU'RE FULL.

DURING THE U.S. CIVIL WAR, LOLLIPOPS WERE SOMETIMES MADE OF HARD CANDY STUCK TO THE END OF A PENCIL.

Scientists
think that
Jupiter
bumped
a planet
out of our solar system
four billion years ago.

A SCIENTIST USED MICROBES IN PETRI DISHES TO RE-CREATE

A FAMOUS VINCENT VAN GOGH PAINTING.

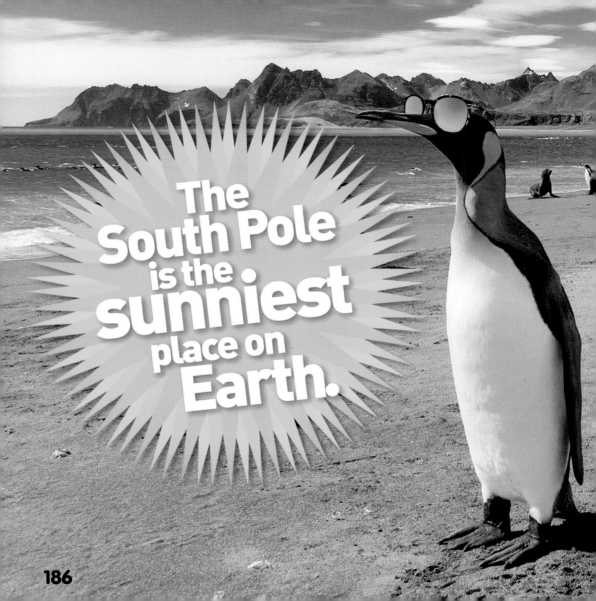

The South Pole is the **sunniest** place on Earth.

Scientists nicknamed a new species of **peacock spider** **Sparklemuffin.**

The Caspian Sea is actually a lake.

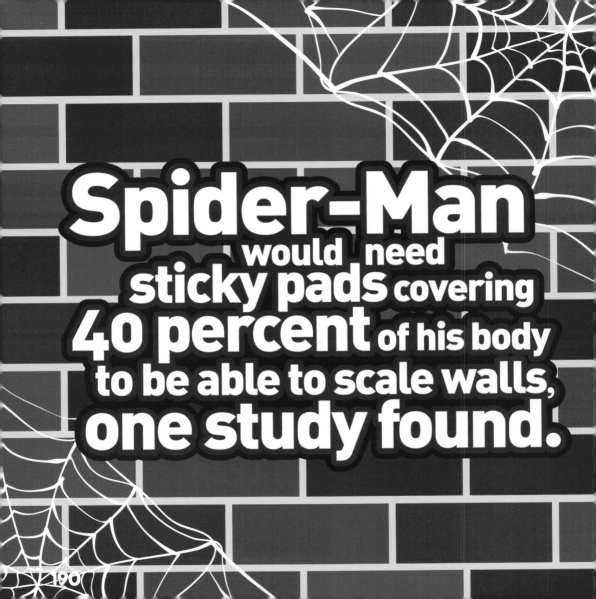

Spider-Man would need **sticky pads** covering **40 percent** of his body to be able to scale walls, **one study found.**

RESIDENTS OF BARNAUL, SIBERIA, **CAMPAIGNED TO ELECT A CAT AS THEIR MAYOR.**

The narrowest street in the world is only **one foot wide.** (0.3 m)

A KID HAD A LEGO PIECE STUCK UP HIS NOSE FOR THREE YEARS.

191

Cuttlefish
hold their breath
when **threatened**
by **predators.**

AN ASTEROID NAMED **SPOOKY** FLEW PAST EARTH ON HALLOWEEN.

THE EARLIEST VERSION OF THE **PENNY** SAID "**MIND YOUR BUSINESS**," NOT "**IN GOD WE TRUST.**"

IT COSTS 1.5 CENTS TO MAKE A PENNY.

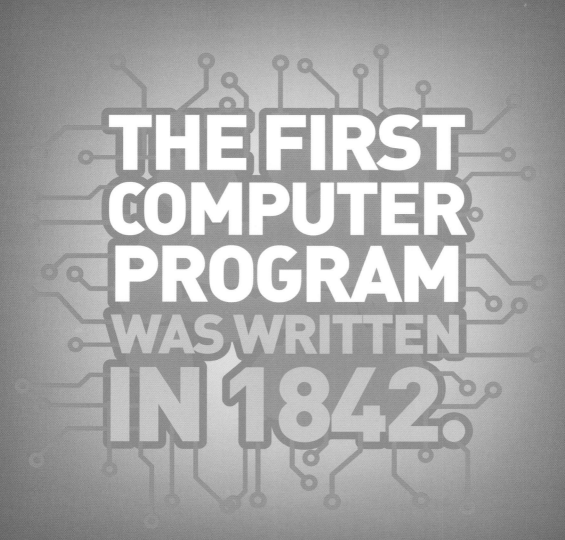

THE FIRST
COMPUTER
PROGRAM
WAS WRITTEN
IN 1842.

196

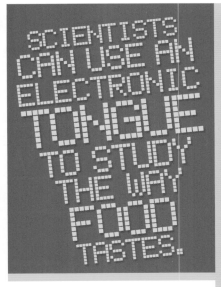

SCIENTISTS CAN USE AN ELECTRONIC TONGUE TO STUDY THE WAY FOOD TASTES.

JELLYFISH GOO CAN BE USED TO GENERATE ENERGY.

THE MOST SELFIES TAKEN IN THREE MINUTES = 134

SOME OF THE

first
vacuum
cleaners
WERE SO LARGE
THEY HAD TO BE DELIVERED BY A
horse-drawn • **carriage.**

A dog drove his owner's truck into a lake in Maine, U.S.A. (No one was injured.)

Some scientists think the **moon** is a **broken-off piece of Earth.**

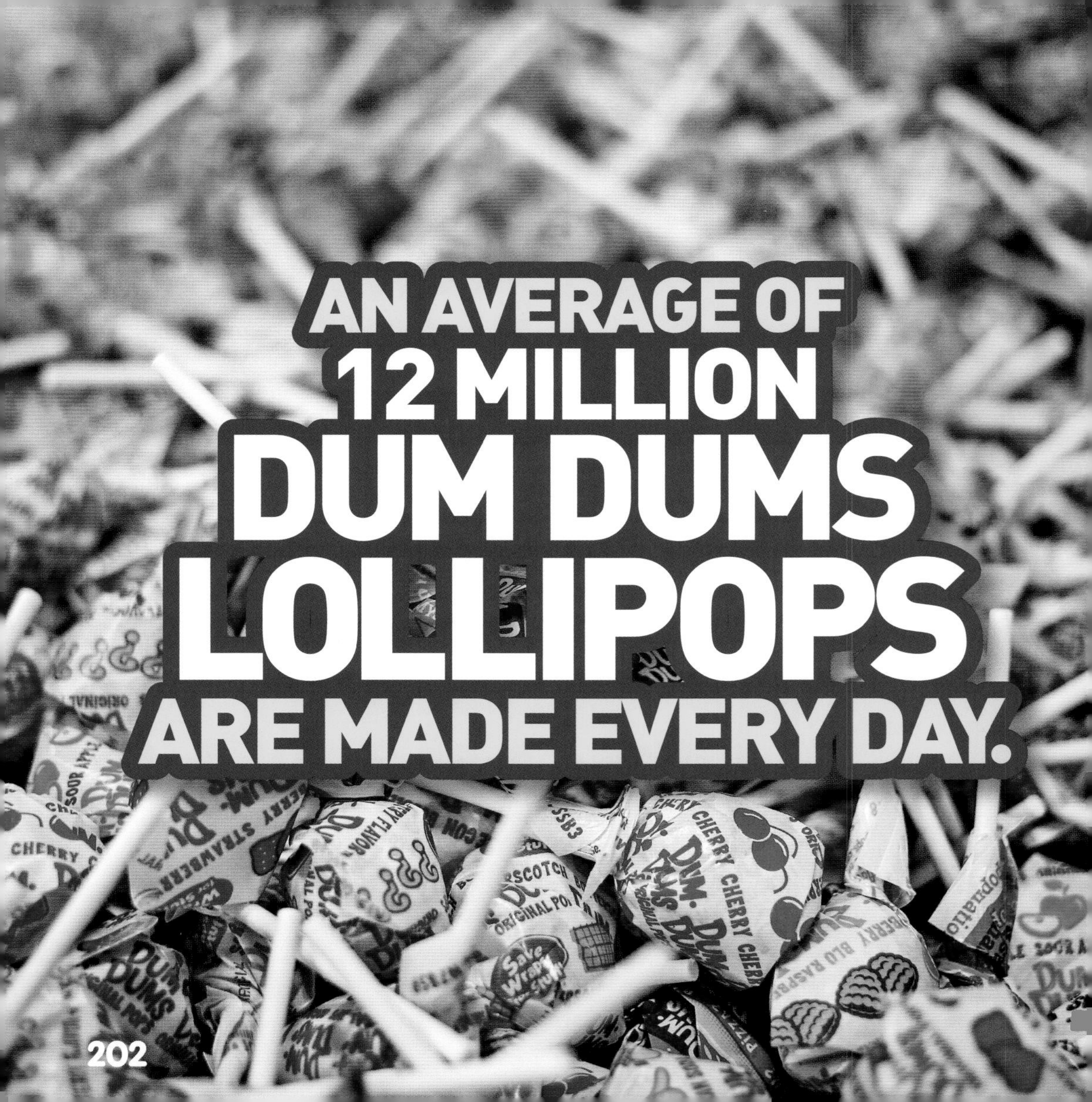

AN AVERAGE OF
12 MILLION
DUM DUMS
LOLLIPOPS
ARE MADE EVERY DAY.

THE HAIRS ON **RASPBERRIES**

ARE CALLED **STYLES.**

The **land area** of the Riyadh, Saudi Arabia, **airport** is bigger than the city of Washington, D.C.

A commonly used **medicine** was developed from **mold** found in **sewer water.**

IT IS ILLEGAL IN SWITZERLAND TO OWN JUST ONE GUINEA PIG.

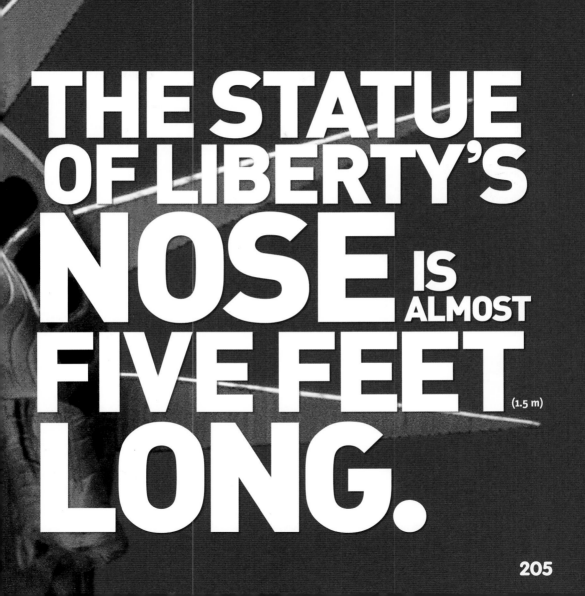

THE STATUE OF LIBERTY'S NOSE IS ALMOST FIVE FEET (1.5 m) LONG.

THE WORLD'S LARGEST COLLECTION OF FOSSILIZED POOP: 1,277 INDIVIDUAL PIECES.

THERE IS A GELATO MUSEUM IN ITALY.

IN CALIFORNIA, U.S.A., THERE IS A MUSEUM DEDICATED ENTIRELY TO BANANAS.

A MUSEUM IN OREGON, U.S.A., HAS A COLLECTION OF 300 VACUUMS.

207

GUESS WHAT?

Sometimes even sticky syrup won't slow you down!
WHEN?

Hanging around cows might keep you from itching!
HOW?

WANNA FIND OUT?

If you want to cool down, yawn!
WHY?

The FUN doesn't have to end here! Find these far-out facts and more in *Weird But True! 9.*

NATIONAL GEOGRAPHIC KIDS

weird but true! 9
350 OUTRAGEOUS FACTS
That's Weird!

NATIONAL GEOGRAPHIC KiDS

AVAILABLE WHEREVER BOOKS ARE SOLD
Get a fun freebie at natgeokids.com/fun-pack

FACTFINDER

Boldface indicates illustrations.

A

Aglets 80, **80**
Airplanes 138, 158
Algae 165
Allergies 31
Almonds 70, **70**
Amazon River, South America 124
Ants 20, **20**, 84, **84**
Apples **142–143**, 143
Apps, toilet rental 25
Arctic regions 84
Arica, Chile 140
Art
 gumball art 173, **173**
 Lego Batmobile 78, **78–79**
 petri dishes 185, **185**
 toast art 145, **145**
 yarn-covered bus **98–99**, 99
Asteroids 194, **194**
Asthma 180
Astronomers 25, 120
Atlantic City, New Jersey, U.S.A. 43
Australia 109

B

Babies, naming 65
Baboons (lemons) 90
Bacteria 71, 106, 179, **179**
Bananas 89, **89**, 144, **144**, 207, **207**
Barf and barfing 9, **9**, 132
Barnaul, Siberia, Russia 191
Baseball 111, **111**, 134, 170, **170**,
 178, **178**

Batmobile 78, **78–79**
Bats 37, **37**, 45, 125, **125**
Batteries 127, **127**
Bears 84, 96, **96**
Beavers, parachuting 19, **19**
Bed, reading in 53, **53**
Bees 66–67, **67**
Bicycles 60, **60–61**
Bird poop 84
Birds
 eaten by carnivorous plants 39
 eaten by spiders 164
 fossils 124
 problem solving 124
 tap dancing 121, **121**
Black holes 13
Bladder, full 90
Blimps 71
Blinking 108, **108**
Blood 154, 165
Blue (color) 167, **167**
Bo (dog) 134, **134**
Boats, early 13
Bones: in feet 50, **50**
Bonobos **86–87**, 87
Boston Bruins 51
Boxing 111
Brain, animal 47, 75, 155
Brain, human 39, 112, **112**, 120, **120**,
 183
Brown bats 37, **37**
Bubbles 130, **130–131**
Bugs: in your house 159
Buses **98–99**, 99

C

California, U.S.A. 65, 207
Camel milk 97, **97**
Cancer: detection by pigeons 171,
 171
Candy corn 108–109, **109**
Carnivorous plants 39
Cars
 Lego Batmobile 78, **78–79**
 most expensive 113
 recycled 122–123, **122–123**
 snowmobile 62, **62**
 taxis 85, **85**
Caspian Sea 189, **189**
Castle, medieval 157
Cat: as mayor 191
Caterpillars 90, **90**
Chameleons 108
Cheese, moldy 133, **133**
"Chicken wing" (golf swing) 71
Chickens 109, **109**
Children
 allergies 31
 asthma 180
 growth 83
Chili peppers 165, **165**
Chimpanzees 165, **165**
China 88, 139, 157
Chinese giant salamanders 97, **97**
Chocolate 51, **51**, 68, **68**, 85, 140, **140**
Civil War, U.S. 183
Claus, Santa 94
Climate change 84
Cockroaches 47, **47**, 166, **166**
Coconut crabs 84, **84**

FACTFINDER

Coffee 18
Columbus, Christopher 65
Comets 68, **68**
Computers 88, **88**, 196
Corgis 164
Corn 53, **53**
Corn mazes 172, **172**
Corpus Christi, Texas, U.S.A. 84
Cowboy hats 121, **121**
Cranberries 57, **57**
Crocodile eggs 44
Cuttlefish **192–193**, 193

D

Dancing 121, **121**, 152, **152**, 176
Darth Vader (character) 11, **11**
Death metal music 76
Deserts 85, 135, **135**
Diamonds 15, 36
Dinosaurs 38, **38**, 84, 152, **152**
Dishwashing 31
Disneyland, California, U.S.A. 147
Divers and diving 11, **104–105**
Dogs
    and asthma 180
    on baseball card 134
    corgis 164
    dogsledding 126, **126**
    driving truck 200, **200**
    musical canine freestyle 74, **74**
    poodles 126, **126**
    smell of paws 51
    talking to, in "baby voice" 85
Dominoes 106, **106**
Dorado catfish 124, **124**

Doughnuts **54–55**, 55, 88
Dragonflies 13, **13**
Dreams and dreaming 129, 150
Droughts 168
Duels 25
Dum Dums lollipops 202, **202**

E

Earmuffs 74, **74**, 179
Earth (planet)
    atmosphere 124
    broken-off piece 201
    changing shape 82
    distance to moon 166
    first living things 106
    magnetic field 45
    moving away from sun 119
    number of trees 35
    undiscovered species 177
    water 116, 124
Earthquakes 4, 120
Earworms 106
Easter bunny 84
Eels 45, **45**
Eggs 14, 44, 46, **46**, 72–73, **72–73**
Einstein, Albert 74, 97
Electronic tongue 197
Elephants 48–49, **48–49**, 70, **70**
Emotions 88, 145
England 96, 150, 157
Everest, Mount, China-Nepal 4, **4–5**

F

Fast food 159
Feathers 84, **84**

Feet, human 50, **50**
Fevers: in plants 94
Fidgeting 80
Fingernails on chalkboard 44
Firefighters 124
Fish scales 80
Flags 147
Fossils 124, 157, 163, 206, **206**
"Fried egg" (golf term) 72–73
Frogs 14, **14**, 84, 89
Froot Loops cereal 37, **37**
Fungi 15

G

Garfield, James A. 47
Gas, passing 45, 68
Gelato 206, **206**
Giraffes 156, **156**
Glaciers 124
Global warming 82
Glow-in-the-dark turtles 153, **153**
Gluteus maximus 127
Goats **54**, 55
Golf 67, **72**, 72–73, 77, **77**
Grass: as dental floss 30
Grima 44
Guinea pigs 203, **203**
Gumball art 173, **173**
Gut, human 20, 183, **183**

H

Hair 39, 66, 139, **139**
Halloween 194
Ham 146, **146**
Hamburgers 159

Harvard University 144
Hawks 39
Hearing, sense of 32, 33
Heart surgery 26, **26**
Hedgehogs 45
Henry III, King (England) 96
Hershey's kisses 157, **157**
Hitchcock, Alfred 46
Hockey 51
Hockey, underwater **16–17,** 17
Honey **66–67,** 67
Honeybees 66, **66**
Horses **100,** 132, **132,** 198, **198–199**
Hubble Space Telescope 27, **27**
Hula hoops 171, **171**
Human body
    blinking 108, **108**
    bones in feet 50, **50**
    brain 39, 112, **112,** 120, **120,** 183
    gut 20, 183, **183**
    hair 139, **139**
    heart surgery 26, **26**
    largest muscle 127
    philtrum 160–161, **160–161**
    sleep 118, 129
    smell 18, 75
    taste buds 114
    toes 150, **150**
Humming: by giraffes 156, **156**
Hummingbirds 39, **39**

I

Ice: prehistoric viruses 25
Ice cream 42
Ice-skating 136, **136–137**

Idaho, U.S.A. 19, **19**
Iditarod (sled dog race) 126, **126**
In-flight menus 138
Insects: 3-D glasses 30, **30**
International Year of Light (2015) 42
Italy 206

J

Jabba the Hutt (character) 167, **167**
Jack-go-to-bed-at-noon (plant) 44
Jelly beans 151, **151,** 179, **179**
Jellyfish 24, **24,** 197
Jet packs, water-powered 124
Jousting 100, **100**
Juggling 133
Jupiter (planet) 184, **184**

K

Kangaroos 6, **6**
Kansas, U.S.A. 103, **103**
Kellogg Company 37
Kissing: prairie dogs **92–93,** 93
Komodo dragons 165

L

Left-handedness 18
Lego bricks 78, **78–79,** 191, **191**
Lemons 65, **65,** 90
Leo X, Pope 48–49
Liberia 134
"Liberty Cabbage" 138, **138**
Librocubicularists 53, **53**
Light signals 175
Lightbulbs 39
Lightning 21, **21**

Lincoln, Abraham 39, 111
Lips, smelling with 71
Lollipops 183, **183,** 202, **202**
Los Angeles, California, U.S.A. 168,
    168–169
Luke Skywalker (character) 10, **10**
Lying 90

M

Magnetic fields 45
Maine, U.S.A. 200, **200**
Mammals
    peeing 15
    pooping 164
Mantis shrimp **174–175,** 175
Mars (planet) 52, **52,** 91, **91**
Maryland, U.S.A. 100, **100,** 172, **172**
Massachusetts, U.S.A. 7, **7,** 140, 176
Math 25
Maya pyramid **148–149**
Medicine
    antibiotics 165
    ants 20
    from cockroaches 47
    human spit as 9
    from mold 203
    from rain forest plants 69
Mercury (planet) 9
Metal, world's lightest 159, **159**
Metric system 134
Mexico 124, 148–149, **148–149**
Miami, Florida, U.S.A. 164
Micro-robots 6
Microbes 183, **183,** 185, **185**
Microlattice 159, **159**

FACTFINDER

Milk, camel 97, **97**
Minnesota, U.S.A. 12, **12**, 85
M&M's 171, **171**
Mold 203, **203**
"Mona Lisa" 145, **145**
Money 68, 146, **146**, 195, **195**
Monopoly (board game) 43, **43**
Moon 201, **201**
Moonbows 40–41, **40–41**
Mosquitoes 37, **37**, 75, **75**
Muscles 90, 127
Museums 125, 206–207, **206–207**
Mushrooms 28, **28–29**, 127, **127**
Music 76, 88, 106
Musical canine freestyle 74, **74**
Musicians: reaction times 44
Mussels 45
Myanmar 134

N

Naked mole rats 125, **125**
Names, baby 65
National Moldy Cheese Day 133
Native Americans 166
Neanderthals 30
New England clam chowder 140, **140**
New Mexico State University 33
New Zealand 65, 77, 84, 128
North Pole 21
North Pole, Alaska, U.S.A. 94
Noses 25, **25**, 191, **191**, **204–205**, 205
Nuclear power plants 24

O

Obama, Barack 134

Oceans 104–105, **104–105**, 182
Octopuses 154–155, **154–155**, 164, **164**
Oklahoma, U.S.A. 102
Olympic Games 64, **64**, 69
Onions 163
Onoway, Canada 44
Ontario, Canada 136, **136–137**
Orchids 75, **75**
Oregon, U.S.A. 207
Oxygen 125, 128

P

Paddling: in pumpkin 7, **7**
Painting 69
Pancakes 20, **20**, 59, **59**
Paper, oldest 141, **141**
Parachuting: by beavers 19, **19**
Parrots 45, **45**
Peach pits, fossilized 157
Peacock spiders 188, **188**
Pee and peeing 15, 30
Peekaboo 115
Pencils: as lollipop sticks 183, **183**
Penguins 84, **84**, 186–187, **186–187**
Pennies 195, **195**
Penny farthings 60, **60–61**
Petri dishes 185, **185**
Pharaohs, female 47, **47**
Phelps, Michael 64, **64**
Philtrum 160–161, **160–161**
Phloem 89, **89**
Pigeons **124**, 171, **171**
Pigs 8, 8
Pilots 138
Pink lemonade 153

Pips 106, **106**
Pizza 81, **81**, 144, **144**
Plano, Texas, U.S.A. 166
Plants
    boats made from 13
    carnivorous 39
    on diamond deposits 36
    fevers 94
    learning 77
    medicine from 69
    sense of hearing 33
    talking to one another 15
Plastic: oceans 182
Pluto (dwarf planet) 114
Pollination 66–67
Poodles 126, **126**
Poop 84, 159, 164, 206, **206**
Portugal 44
Postage stamps 144, **144**
Potato, duck-shaped 150, **150**
Prairie dogs **92–93**, 93
Presidents of the United States
    Abraham Lincoln 39, 111
    Barack Obama 134
    James A. Garfield 47
    Ronald Reagan 151, **151**
    Theodore Roosevelt 39
    Woodrow Wilson 110
Pumpkins 7, **7**, 101, **101**
Puppets 167, **167**
Purple (color) 62, **62**
Pyramids 148–149, **148–149**

R

Rain 94, **94**, 140

Rain forest plants 69, **69**
Rainbows 40–41, **40–41**
Raindrops 20
Raspberries (fruit) 203, **203**
Raspberries (sound) 87
Reading: in bed 53, **53**
Reagan, Ronald 151, **151**
Recycled cars 122–123, **122–123**
Redondo Beach, California, U.S.A. 71
Reptiles, ancient flying 139, **139**
Reservoirs 168, **168–169**
Restaurants 109
Rhampholeon spinosus 108
Ribs, human 106
Rice 56, **56**
Rings 39, **39**
Riyadh, Saudi Arabia 203
Roadkill 179
Robots 6, 26, **26**, 59, **59**, 66–67
Rock music 88
Rocks 52, **52**
Roller coasters 115, **115**
Roosevelt, Theodore 39
Rugby 42, **42**
Running 63
Rushmore, Mount, South Dakota,
        U.S.A. 125
Ruth, Babe 170, **170**

S
Sahara, Africa 135, **135**
Salamanders 97, **97**
Sand Museum, Tottori, Japan 125
Saskatchewan, Canada 55
Saturn (planet) 44

Sauerkraut 138, **138**
Scotland 133, 176, **176**
Scuba diving 11
Sea anemones 45
Sea bunnies (slugs) 114, **114**
Sea turtles 162, **162**
Selfies: world record 197
Sewer water 203
"Shade balls" 168, **168–169**
Sharks 8, 76, **76**, 135, **135**
Sheep 58, **58**, 110, **110–111**
Shoelaces 80, **80**
Shrimp **174–175**, 175
Siberia (region), Russia 25, 191
Skin, artificial 45
Skywalker hoolock gibbons 44
Sleep 118, 129
Slime 84, **84**
Smell, sense of 71
Smells 163
Snails 71, **71**
Snakes 45, 68, 112, **112**
Snickers bars 132
Snoods 80, **80**
Snorkel gear **16–17**, 17
Snow 124, 133
Snowmobiles 62, **62**
Soap bubble, world's largest 130,
        130–131
Socks 74, **74**
Solar-powered devices 85
Sound waves 75, 119
Sour Patch Kids 121
South Africa 89
South Pole 21, 186

Space
    asteroids 194, **194**
    black holes 13
    body of water 59
    comets 68, **68**
    diamonds from 15
    Jupiter 184, **184**
    Mars 52, **52**, 91, **91**
    Mercury 9
    Pluto 114
    Saturn 44
    star dust 33
    sun 107, **107**, 119
    Venus 164, **164**
Space hamburgers 164, **164**
Space telescope 27, **27**
Spam 138
Sparklemuffin (spider) 188, **188**
Speeding tickets 69
Spiciness 88
Spider-Man 190
Spiders 77, 88, 115, 164, 188, **188**
Spiderwebs 77, **190**
Spit, human 9
Spooky (asteroid) 194, **194**
Springtime 83
Squirrel soup 47
Squirrels 65
Stanley Cup 51
Star dust 33
"The Star-Spangled Banner" 176
Star Wars (movies) 10–11, **10–11**, 44,
        167, **167**
Starburst candies 132
Stars 13, 164

FACTFINDER

Statue of Liberty **204–205**, 205
Stethoscopes 164, **164**
Street, world's narrowest 191, **191**
Styles (raspberry hairs) 203, **203**
Sun 107, **107**, 119
Sunlight 84, 186, **186–187**
Swift, Taylor 173, **173**
Swim fins 63, **63**
Swimming 64, **64**
Swimsuits: for turtles 162, **162**
Switzerland 203

T

T. rex 38, **38**
Tasmanian devils 22, **22–23**
Taste buds 114
Taxis 85, **85**
Teeth 30, 49, 80
Temples 124
Ten-gallon hats 121, **121**
Termites 84
Thames River, England 96
Thanksgiving dinner 44, **44**
3-D glasses 30, **30**
3-D printing 106
Titanic, R.M.S. 176
Toadstools 28, **28–29**
Toast art 145, **145**
Toenail clippings 144
Toes 150, **150**
Toilet rentals 25
Tomatoes 62, **62**
Tonga 144
Tongues 108, 197
Tooth enamel 80

Toothbrushes 167, **167**
Tornadoes 95, **95**
Touch, sense of 150
Tractor beams 119
Trees **34–35**, 35, 140, **140**
Trucks 163, **163**, 200, **200**
Turkey (country) 18, 37
Turkeys (birds) 80, **80**, 166
Turnips 127
Turtles 153, **153**, 162, **162**
Twitter 109

U

Underwater hockey **16–17**, 17
Underwater volcanoes 135, **135**
United States
  Civil War 183
  flag 147
  food eaten 127, 144
  and metric system 134
  most recycled product 123
  names of towns 128
  relative size 135
  World War I 138
UPS drivers 45
Urine 15, 30

V

Vacuum cleaners 198, **198–199**, 207, **207**
Van Gogh, Vincent 185, **185**
Vanilla 51, **51**
Vatican **48**, 48–49
Vegetables: fertilized by urine 30
Venus (planet) 164, **164**

Virga (rain) 94, **94**
Viruses 9, 25, 84
Volcanoes, underwater 135, **135**
Vomit, fake 9

W

Water
  floating in space 59
  molecules 6
  pink tap water 44
  safe for human use 116
Waterfalls 12, **12**
Watermelons 102, **102**
Whale fossils 163
Wheat 103, **103**
Whistling 37
White House, Washington, D.C.
  110–111, **110–111**
Wilson, Woodrow 110
Wires 158
Wolves 32, **32**
Words and letters 44, 97, 133, 165
World War I 138
World's Fair (1904) 70, **70**
Worms 75, **75**, 84, 125, 176, **176**
Wounds, human spit for 9

Y

Yarn 98, **98–99**

PHOTO CREDITS

215

Since 1888, the National Geographic Society has funded more than 12,000 research, exploration, and preservation projects around the world. The Society receives funds from National Geographic Partners, LLC, funded in part by your purchase. A portion of the proceeds from this book supports this vital work. To learn more, visit natgeo.com/info.

NATIONAL GEOGRAPHIC and Yellow Border Design are trademarks of the National Geographic Society, used under license.

For more information, visit nationalgeographic .com, call 1-800-647-5463, or write to the following address:
National Geographic Partners
1145 17th Street N.W.
Washington, D.C. 20036-4688 U.S.A.

Visit us online at nationalgeographic.com/books

For librarians and teachers:
ngchildrensbooks.org

More for kids from National Geographic:
kids.nationalgeographic.com

For information about special discounts for bulk purchases, please contact National Geographic Books Special Sales:
specialsales@natgeo.com

For rights or permissions inquiries, please contact National Geographic Books Subsidiary Rights: bookrights@natgeo.com

Designed by Rachel Hamm Plett, Moduza Design

First edition published 2016
Reissued and updated 2018

Paperback ISBN: 978-1-4263-3118-3
Reinforced library binding ISBN:
978-1-4263-3119-0

Printed in China
18/PPS/1

The publisher would like to thank Jen Agresta, project manager; Avery Hurt, researcher; Jeanette Swain, researcher; Stephanie Drimmer, researcher; Kate Hale, project editor; Paige Towler, project manager; Julide Dengel, art director; Kathryn Robbins, art director; Ruthie Thompson; art designer; Lori Epstein, photo director; Hillary Leo, photo editor; Alix Inchausti, production editor; Anne LeongSon and Gus Tello, production assistants.